Couples Game Night Challenge

Couples challenge for you and your loved one *or* for couples game night

Cheryl Pryor

Arlington & Amelia

First Printing

ISBN:10-1-886541-18-3
ISBN:13-978-1-886541-18-4

FOR HOLLY AND JUSTIN

CONTENTS

How To Use This Book

If you're looking for a fun way to see how much you really know about your loved one this book is a fun and entertaining way to do so. The way the book is designed is you can use it for just you and your loved one or have friends over for game night and set it up as a couples challenge.

You will find your memory and your knowledge tested on just how much you really know about each other while having a great time. This book keeps it light and entertaining while at the same time asks some pretty challenging questions.

Here's how it works for couples only.

If you are using this just for the two of you there are several ways of completing the book. Rather than a fill-in-the blank where you both take turns, you can instead quiz each other and hear each other's answers instantaneously. No time to sit and contemplate your answers, these aren't deep probing questions meant to do anything other than to entertain and yet just maybe you'll find out a little more about each other at the same time.

If you are together while taking the quiz you can take turns asking each other questions or you can write your answers down and compare each other's answers; but it's much more fun to do this together while interacting and you can then discuss your answers with each other. The questions that have he/she or his/hers, for example:

If he/she were stranded on a desert island, name one thing they would wish they could have on the island with them – besides you.

On those questions you can either alternate answering how he would answer, the next time you come across a he/she question answer it how she would answer, or answer each of those questions both ways. First answer it how he would answer and the second time how she would answer.

Here's how it works as a couples game challenge.

Are you having a get together with some of your friends who are also couples and want to have a bit of a competition and fun at the same time.

The first half of the couples *(men on one side and women on the other)* are seated together on one side and the other half of the couples are seated facing their mates. Place them with space in between, far enough where they can't read while their mate is answering the questions or can overhear any comments made.

Set this up where the women are asked the questions about their husbands or boyfriends and then switch it around.

When you come across the questions that have he/she or his/hers for example:

If he/she were stranded on a desert island, name one thing they would wish they could have on the island with them – besides you.

On the he/she or his/her questions when playing with couples you can answer depending on which group is answering first. If the women are answering the question first have them answer how he would answer, for example: *If he were stranded on a desert island...,* when the men are answering first have them answer the question how she would answer, for example: *If she were stranded on a desert island... .*

You can purchase dry erase boards at a dollar store and give each person one (even with 3 – 4 couples that's less than $10) or use index cards (preferably the larger ones so they are easy enough to read) to write your answers.

Ask everyone the question at the same time and both sides mark their answers down and then compare anwers when called on. The first half of couple #1 shows their answer first and then their mate shows their answer and then on to the next couple with the host keeping score. Scores for each question are given at the beginning of each category.

Keep score and at the end of the night give out a prize for the couple who scored the highest and maybe a different type prize for the one who got the lowest score as a gag gift.

There are 5 questions in each category with 25 different categories. There are different ways of choosing your questions. You can ask one question from each category which would give you 25 questions in all, choose 5 categories and ask all the questions from each of those categories, or just pick and choose questions throughout the book. If you want to limit your time you can preset a winning score, for example the first couple to score 100 points wins.

If you are going to just pick and choose questions throughout the book the host of the party may want to do this ahead of time to keep the game flowing.

There are enough questions to play the game 5 different times or more as a couples challenge. If you're going to play again with the same group you may want to mark the questions asked so next time you play you don't repeat the questions but start with a new group of challenging questions.

If there is an odd man out at the party they can be the game host and ask the questions and keep score, otherwise choose a scorekeeper and one person can be in charge of asking the questions (usually the host of the party) to keep it running smoothly.

There is one rule I would suggest when you use this as a couples game challenge. If anyone is uncomfortable at all in answering a certain question they can have the option of passing and just skip that question and go on to the next one. No questions asked, no pressure – but; they can't pass merely because they don't know the answer. It has to be due to being a bit too personal and information they are uncomfortable in sharing. Be sure this rule is made clear ahead of time and no one from either side should pressure them into answering something they are uncomfortable with.

The questions are light enough to make it fun for a party and aren't meant to be deep, probing thought provoking questions even though there are some that are pretty challenging questions. If you are looking for a deeper more meaningful relationship quiz just for the two of you, you will find that in my book *'How Much Do You REALLY Know About The Love Of Your Life.'*

Remember this game is for you and your loved one or for you and your friends to share laughter and good times – not to start any fights. Don't embarrass your loved one and don't give away secrets you know they wouldn't otherwise share. The couples challenge is a great way to fill time at a party and have lots of fun and laughter with your friends, too.

1

HOW WELL DO YOU *REALLY* KNOW YOUR LOVED ONE

1. If your loved one could pick any time era to live in; when would it be

2. They say men marry women like their mother: How are you similar to his mother

3. If he/she were stranded on a desert island, name one thing they would wish they could have on the island with them – besides you

4. If he/she could have plastic surgery; what body

part would they most like to change

5. If he/she could choose any job – what would be
their dream job

2

DO YOU REMEMBER

SCORE: 10 POINTS FOR EACH CORRECT ANSWER IN THIS CATEGORY

1. A nickname he/she had when growing up

2. A story of his/her childhood they told you about

3. How old was he/she when you got married

4. What time of the day or evening did you get married

5. What was the last thing you fought about

3

A FIRST TIME FOR EVERYTHING

SCORE: 5 POINTS FOR EACH CORRECT ANSWER IN THIS CATEGORY

1. Where did you go on your first date with each other?

2. Where were you when you first kissed?

3. Who said I love you first?

4. What is the first gift he or she bought for you?

5. How long did you know him/her when you first met his/her family

4

IN THE BEGINNING

SCORE: 10 POINTS FOR EACH CORRECT ANSWER IN THIS CATEGORY

1. How did you meet each other:

   A. *through work*

   B. *through a friend*

   C. *social media*

   D. *introduced ourselves*

2. What is the name of the hospital where he/she was born

3. What city was he/she born

4. What is his/her astrological sign

5. What is his/her birthdate – including the year

5

ROMANCE IS IN THE AIR

SCORE: 5 POINTS FOR EACH CORRECT ANSWER IN THIS CATEGORY

1. How old was he/she when you met

2. On your first date did he:

    A. *strike out*

    B. *get to first base*

    C. *hit a home run*

    D. *grand slam*

3. Name something you always did before you went out on a date with your mate, that you no longer do

4. How long did you date before you saw each other exclusively

5. How long after you knew him/her before you knew "they were the one"

6

SCHOOL DAYS

SCORE: 5 POINTS FOR EACH CORRECT ANSWER IN THIS CATEGORY

1. What was his/her favorite subject in school

2. What was his/her least favorite subject

3. Where did they attend high school...name of school

4. Was he/she ever sent to the principal's office

5. What was their major in college

7

WHICH ONE IS...

1. Which one is the first to go to bed and who is the first one out of bed in the morning.

2. Who is most often late of the two of you

3. Who is most likely to "misplace" their keys, phone, forget about an event...

4. Which one of the two of you has to make an entrance when you go to a party or event

5. Which is the loudest of the two of you

8

WEDDING & HONEYMOON

1. Who proposed & how

2. Name a song played at your wedding (the song you first danced to as husband and wife preferably)

3. Use one word to describe him/her on your wedding day

4. Who caught the bridal bouquet/garter

5. What was your favorite wedding gift

9

FINISH THIS SENTENCE

SCORE: 10 POINTS FOR EACH CORRECT ANSWER IN THIS CATEGORY

1. The first thing he/she does in the morning is

_____.

2. He/She drives me crazy when _____.

3. How would your loved one complete these

sentences:

I hate to be _____. He/she hates to be

_____.

4. How would your loved one complete these
sentences:

I am scared of _____. He/she is scared of

_____.

5. How would your loved one complete this sentence:

If I could change anything about myself, I would

change _____.

10

FAVORITES OF HIS & HERS

1. What is your favorite body part of his/hers

2. What is his/her favorite TV show

3. What is his/her favorite movie

4. What is his/her favorite way to spend "free" time

5. What is your favorite thing he/she does to make you feel special

11

ENTERTAINMENT

SCORE: 5 POINTS FOR EACH CORRECT ANSWER IN THIS CATEGORY

1. What is his/her favorite book

2. What is his/her favorite type of music

3. What is his/her favorite place to go to hang out with friends

4. What is his/her favorite movie star

5. What is his/her favorite sport

12

WHAT WOULD YOU DO

SCORE: 10 POINTS FOR EACH CORRECT ANSWER IN THIS CATEGORY

1. Your house is on fire: you have saved all family members and pets. What is the one other thing you would save if you had time to get one more thing?

2. If your loved one found a $20 bill; what would he/she spend it on

3. You have just finished building a time machine and you know it works. You grab your mate and buckle yourselves in. To what event in history would you go to experience for yourselves

4. You know a friend, or know of a stranger or friend of a friend, who is suffering hard times. What thing would he/she be most likely to do to help this person or family (within reason, something not out of the realm of reality)

5. You are at a family reunion and someone has just told everyone a story about your loved one that you know embarrasses him, what do you do

13

I'LL NEVER FORGET THE TIME

SCORE: 10 POINTS FOR EACH CORRECT ANSWER IN THIS CATEGORY

1. I'll never forget the time we _____

2. Our worst vacation was _____

3. The most special time in our life so far was when

_____

4. He/She really surprised me when

_____

5. Something really special a friend did for us that

meant a lot to both of us was when _____

14

HOW OBSERVANT ARE YOU

1. What kind of cologne/perfume does he/she wear

2. Without looking: What is he/she wearing now

3. What month did you meet

4. What is the color of his/her toothbrush

5. What is the color of his/her favorite shirt/top

15

WHEN YOU DON'T ALWAYS SEE EYE TO EYE

SCORE: 5 POINTS FOR EACH CORRECT ANSWER IN THIS CATEGORY

1. What is the one thing he/she has too much of

2. If he/she could throw away one thing that belonged to you, what would it be

3. What is the one thing you wish he/she would get rid of

4. You're going out on date night, dinner and to a movie. He wants to see the latest adventure flick, she wants to see a chick flick. Which movie would you

most likely end up at

5. You have just met a new couple that wants to hang out with you and your mate. You can't stand them, your mate thinks they are a lot of fun. What do you do

16

DO YOU AGREE

1. Who is the funniest of the two of you

2. Who is the better driver of the two of you

3. If you were given the choice to live anywhere in the world, where would it be and does your loved one feel the same way about moving there

4. If someone told you they were going to give you a gift card for $1,000 and just tell them the name of the store you wanted it from, which store would you choose? Would your mate come up with the same

store?

5. If you offered your mate a choice of restaurants to go, what would they pick:

    A. Italian / Mediterranean

    B. Mexican

    C. Chinese / Thai / Sushi

    D. American: Burgers / BBQ / Fried Chicken

17

RELATIONSHIPS

1. Which video game best describes you:

A. *Need For Speed*

B. *Sims*

C. *Nintendogs*

D. *Final Fantasy*

2. Which one of your friends would you be least likely to share a secret with

3. Does he/she spend more time looking at the screen of his/her smartphone or at you

4. If one of you was a Democrat and the other a Republican or a Libertarian: would that affect your relationship. How would you solve the issue

5. Which TV show best describes your relationship:

   A. *Parenthood*

   B. *Ozzie & Harriet*

   C. *Friends*

   D. *The Brady Bunch*

   E. *Everybody Loves Raymond*

18

CHARACTER FLAWS

SCORE: 5 POINTS FOR EACH CORRECT ANSWER IN THIS CATEGORY

1. Of the two of you, who has more of a tendency to think they're right all the time

2. Does he/she forgive and forget or hold a grudge

3. Who has to get in the last word in an argument

4. Who is the most jealous of the two of you

5. Who is the biggest spendthrift of the two of you

19

CHARACTER ASSETS

SCORE: 5 POINTS FOR EACH CORRECT ANSWER IN THIS CATEGORY

1. Of the two of you, who is the bigger extrovert

2. What is one thing you really admire about him/her

3. After a fight, who makes the first gesture to make up

4. Tell a kind act he/she did for someone else

5. When you don't feel well or are just plain tired, what kind gesture do they do to make you feel better

20

IT'S ALL ABOUT HER

SCORE: 10 POINTS FOR EACH CORRECT ANSWER IN THIS CATEGORY

1. What kind of animal does she most remind you of:

   A. *kitten*

   B. *K-9 dog*

   C. *pig*

   D. *lemming*

   E. *lamb*

   F. *racehorse*

2. I think her most admirable trait is _____

3. She hates it when I _____

4. If she was a Super Hero, what would her super powers be

5. What Super Hero does she most remind you of

21

IT'S ALL ABOUT HIM

SCORE: 10 POINTS FOR EACH CORRECT ANSWER IN THIS CATEGORY

1. What kind of animal does he most remind you of:

A. *wild stallion*

B. *teddy bear*

C. *pig*

D. *myna bird*

E. *lemming*

F. *sloth*

2. I think his most admirable trait is _____

3. He hates it when I _____.

4. If he was a Super Hero, what would his super hero name be

5. What Super Hero does he most remind you of

22

TEST YOUR MEMORY

*SCORE: 10 POINTS FOR EACH CORRECT ANSWER IN
THIS CATEGORY*

1. What is his/her most overused expression

2. What is the first meal he/she ever cooked for you

3. Do you know his/her social security # by memory.
Don't say it! Just answer yes or no – *truthfully!*

4. What story have you told him/her tell over and
over and over again

5. How many charge cards do they have in their
wallet

23

FOOD

1. Name a dish he/she orders OFTEN when you go out for dinner

2. If you served him _____, he/she would most likely push it to the side of the plate and not eat it.

3. Name a food he/she eats you would NEVER eat

4. My favorite dish he/she cooks for me is

_____

5. What recipe that his/her mother used to make for him/her when they were growing up do they brag about the most

24

THINK ABOUT IT

SCORE: 5 POINTS FOR EACH CORRECT ANSWER IN THIS CATEGORY

1. What one characteristic in a person annoys him/her the most

2. Would he/she say you spend more time on social media or communicating with him/her

3. When I talk I feel he/she really listens to what I'm saying. ***True or False***

4. When you call him/her and they answer "Just a minute," what does that mean to you

5. What is the strangest gift he/she has ever given you

25

RANDOM QUESTIONS

*SCORE: 10 POINTS FOR EACH CORRECT ANSWER IN
THIS CATEGORY*

1. What blood type does he/she have

2. Name a person in history your mate admires

3. What would he/she pick as his last meal

4. What celebrity does your mate most resemble

5. Name one thing he/she would have on their
bucket list